THE BOOK OF
SHADOWS

Owner's Personal Record

This book belongs to _____

Birthdate _____Time _____

Place _____Long. & Lat._____

Zodiac Sign _____

Ruling Planet or Planets _____

Astral Color _____

Colors of Harmony _____

Birthstone _____

Jewels to wear for:

   Luck _____

   Health _____

   Fortune _____

Dates of great importance_____

_____

_____

Education_____

Degrees _____

Hobbies or special interest _____

_____

Dates of special events _____

_____

_____

_____

If you become a High Priest or Priestess you may keep
a Coven Record of all the people you teach and also of
all your Coveners.

THE BOOK OF SHADOWS

BY LADY SHEBA

2000
Llewellyn Publications
St. Paul, Minnesota 55164-0383, U.S.A.

First Edition
Third Printing, 2000

Book design and editing by Connie Hill
Cover design by Lisa Novak

Library of Congress Cataloging-in-Publication Data
Bell, Jessie Wicker
    The Book of Shadows / Lady Sheba
        p.   cm. —
    ISBN 0-87542-075-3 (pbk)

Llewellyn Worldwide does not participate in, endorse, or have any authority or responsibility concerning private business transactions between our authors and the public.
    All mail addressed to the author is forwarded but the publisher cannot, unless specifically instructed by the author, give out an address or phone number.

Llewellyn Publications
A Division of Llewellyn Worldwide, Ltd.
P.O. Box 64383, Dept. 0-87542-075-3
St. Paul, MN 55164-0383, U.S.A.
www.llewellyn.com

Printed in the United States of America

Contents

The Book of Shadows

A Message From the Publisher

Lady Sheba's was the first published Book of Shadows in the United States. The author brought it to Llewellyn in 1970; it was released in 1971 and reprinted in 1973.

The impact was enormous. In many ways, this event was the touchstone for Wicca as a religion for the New Age. Yes, it is the "Old Religion," but it also speaks for the re-emergence of the Goddess as women moved beyond the Piscean patriarchy; it speaks for the re-emergence of the Pagan identification with the world of Nature and respect for the environment; and it speaks for the Awakening of the New Age spiritual experience.

Lady Sheba was among the first (perhaps the very first) to register Wicca as a religion (in the State of Michigan) and inspired many others to do the same.

With publication of *The Book of Shadows*—bringing Wicca "out of the closet," Lady Sheba became the target of some animosity. She was accused of violating "oaths of secrecy" and of publishing material that wasn't original with her. She answered that the time for secrecy was past, and that she never claimed to be the author, for this was the Book of Shadows as passed on to her.

In one instance, the Invocation of the Horned God, we want to acknowledge that much longer poetic version was earlier (1965) published and copyrighted by Doreen Valiente in *Pentagram*.

Following publication of *The Grimoire of Lady Sheba* (1972), she withdrew from public life and we lost contact with her. With rumors of her death, and with no contact with the family, we were reluctant to reprint the books. However, this year, following her eightieth birthday, we are again in contact with Lady Sheba and her family, and are re-issuing her works.

Blessed Be,

Carl Llewellyn Weschcke, Publisher

1

THE LAWS

Your High Priestess

In the Magic Circle, the words, commands, and every wish of the High Priestess are law.

She is the earthly, living representative of our Gracious Goddess. She must be obeyed and respected in all things. She is Our Lady and above all others, a queen in the highest sense of the word.

All female coveners must curtsy whenever they come before Her and say, "Blessed Be."

All male coveners must bend the knee and give her a kiss on the right cheek and say, "Blessed Be."

Your High Priest

He is the earthly, living representative of the Great Horned God and in the Magic Circle, He commandeth the respect due to one who is a Magus, a Lord Counselor, and father.

2 / The Laws

The Laws

1. The Law was made and ardane of old.

2. The Law was made for the Wicca to advise and help in their troubles.

3. The Wicca should give due worship to the Gods and obey Their will, which They ardane, for it was made for the good of the Wicca, as the worship of the Wicca is good for the Gods. For the Gods love the brethren of the Wicca.

4. As a man loveth a woman by mastering her,

5. So the Wicca should love the Gods by mastering them.

6. And it is necessary that the Ø (Magic Circle), which is the Temple of the Gods, should be duly cast and purified that it may be a fit place for the Gods to enter.

7. And the Wicca should be properly prepared and purified to enter into the presence of the Gods.

8. With love and worship in their hearts, they shall raise power from their bodies to give power to the Gods.

9. As has been taught of old.

10. For in this way only may man have a communion with the Gods, for the Gods cannot help men without the help of man.

11. And the High Priestess shall rule Her Coven as the representative of the Goddess.

4 / The Laws

12. And the High Priest shall support Her as the representative of the God.

13. And the High Priestess shall choose whom She will, if he have sufficient rank, to be Her High Priest.

14. For, as the God himself kissed Her feet in the Fivefold salute, laying His power at the feet of the Goddess, because of Her youth and beauty, Her sweetness and kindness, Her wisdom and Her justice, Her humility and gentleness and generosity,

15. So He resigned all His power to Her.

16. But the High Priestess should ever mind that all power comes from Him.

17. It is only lent, to be used wisely and justly.

18. And the greatest virtue of a High Priestess be that She recognizes that youth is necessary to the representative of the Goddess.

19. So will She gracefully retire in favor of a younger woman, should the Coven so decide in council.

20. For the true High Priestess realizes that gracefully surrendering the pride of place is one of the greatest virtues.

21. And that thereby will She return to that pride of place in another life, with greater power and beauty.

6 / The Laws

22. In the old days, when Witches extended far, we were free and worshipped in all the greatest temples.

23. But, in these unhappy times, we must celebrate our Sacred Mysteries in secret.

24. So be it ardane, that none but the Wicca may see our mysteries, for our enemies are many and torture loosens the tongue of men.

25. So be it ardane, that no Coven shall know where the next Coven bide.

26. Or who its members be, save only the Priest and Priestess and the Messenger.

27. And there shall be no communication between them, save only by the Messenger of the Gods, or the Summoner.

28. And only if it be safe may the Covens meet in some safe place for the Great Festivals.

29. And while there, none shall say whence they come, nor give their true names.

30. To this end, that if any be tortured, in their agony, they may not tell if they do not know.

31. So be it ardane, that no one shall tell anyone, not of the Craft, who be of the Wicca, or give any names, or where any abide, or in any way tell anything which can betray any of us to our faces.

32. Nor may he tell where the Covendom be.

33. Or the Covenstead.

8 / The Laws

34. Or where the meetings be.

35. And if any break these Laws, even under torture, the Curse of the Goddess shall be upon them, so they may never be reborn on earth, and may they remain where they belong, in the Hell of the Christians.

36. Let each High Priestess govern Her Coven with justice and love, with the help and advice of the High Priest and the Elders, always heeding the advice of the Messenger of the Gods if He comes.

37. She will heed all complaints of all Brothers and strive to settle all differences among them.

38. But it must be recognized that there will always be people who will ever strive to force others to do as they will.

39. These are not necessarily evil.

40. And they oft have good ideas, and such ideas should be talked over in council.

41. But, if they will not agree with their Brothers or if they say:

42. "I will not work under this High Priestess."

43. It hath ever been the Old Law, to be convenient for the Brethren, and to avoid disputes.

44. Any of the third may claim to found a new Coven, because they live over a league from the Covenstead or are about to do so.

45. Anyone living within the Covendom and wishing to form a new Coven shall tell the Elders of their intentions and on the instant avoid their dwelling and remove to a new Covendom.

46. Members of the old Coven may join the new one when it is formed, but if they do they must utterly avoid the old Coven.

47. The Elders of the old and new Covens should meet in peace and brotherly love to decide the new boundaries.

48. Those of the Craft who live outside both Covens may join either indifferent, but not both.

49. Though all may, if the Elders agree, meet for the Great Festivals, if it be truly in peace and brotherly love.

50. But splitting the Coven oft means strife, so for this reason these Laws were made of old, and may the Curse of the Goddess be on any who disregard them!

SO BE IT ARDANE.

51. If you would keep a book (your Black Book) let it be in your own hand of write; let Brothers and Sisters copy what they will, but never let the book out of your hands and never keep the writings of another.

52. For if it be in their hand of write, they may be taken and engained.

53. Let each guard his own writings, and destroy them whenever danger threatens.

54. Learn as much as you may by heart, and when danger is past, rewrite your book an it be safe.

55. For this reason, if any die, destroy their book, an they have not been able to.

56. For, an it be found, 'tis clear proof against them.

57. And our oppressors know well: "Ye may not be a Witch alone."

58. So all their kin and friends be in danger of torture.

59. So destroy everything not necessary.

60. If your book be found on you, 'tis clear proof against you alone. You may be engained.

61. Keep all thoughts of the Craft from your mind.

62. If the torture be too great to bear, say: "I will confess. I cannot bear this torture. What do you want me to say?"

63. If they try to make you talk of the Brotherhood, do not.

64. But if they try to make you speak of impossibilities such as flying through the air, consorting with the Christian Devil, or sacrificing children or eating men's flesh,

65. To obtain relief from the torture, say, "I hold an evil dream, I was beside myself, I was crazed."

66. Not all the magistrates are bad; if there be any excuse, they may show mercy.

67. If you have confessed ought, deny it afterwards. Say you babbled under the torture, say you do not know what you said.

68. If you are condemned, fear not.

69. Fear not, the Brotherhood is powerful, they will help you to escape if you stand steadfast.

70. But if you betray ought, there is no hope for you in this life or that to come.

71. Be sure, if steadfast you go to the pyre, drugs will reach you, you will feel naught. You but go to death and what lies beyond.

The Ecstasy of the Goddess

72. To avoid discovery, let the working tools be as ordinary things that any may have in their houses.

73. Let the Pentacles be of wax so that they may be broken at once or melted.

74. Have no sword, unless your rank allows you one.

75. Have no names or signs on anything.

76. Write the names or signs on them in ink immediately before consecrating them, and wash it off immediately afterwards.

77. Do not engrave them lest they cause discovery.

78. Let the color of the hilts tell which is which.

79. Ever remember, ye are the "Hidden Children of the Goddess," so never do anything to disgrace them or her.

80. Never boast, never threaten, never say you would wish ill of anyone.

81. If any person, not in the magic circle, speak of the Craft say, "Speak not to me of such, it frightens me. 'Tis evil luck to speak of it.'"

82. For this reason: the Christians have their spies everywhere. These speak as if they were well affected to us, as if they would come to our meetings, saying, "My mother used to go to worship the Old Ones. I would I could go myself."

83. To such as these, ever deny all knowledge.

84. But to others, ever say: "'Tis foolish talk of Witches flying through the air. To do so they must be light as thistledown. And men say that Witches all be so bleared-eyed, old crones, so what pleasure can there be at a Witch meeting such as folks talk on?"

85. And say, "Many wise men now say there be no such creatures."

86. Ever make it a jest and in some future time, perhaps, the persecution may die and we may worship our Gods in safety again.

87. Let us all pray for that happy day.

18 / The Laws

88. May the blessings of the Goddess and God be on all those who keep these Laws which are ardane.

89. If the Craft have any Appenage, let all guard it, and help to keep it clear and good for the Craft.

90. And let all justly guard all monies of the Craft.

91. But if any brother truly wrought it, 'tis right they have their pay, and it be just. And this be not taking money for the Art, but for good and honest work.

92. And ever the Christians say, "The laborer is worthy of his hire," but if any brother work willingly for the good of the Craft without pay, 'tis to their greatest honor.

    SO BE IT ARDANE.

93. If there be any quarrels or disputes among the brethren, the High Priestess shall straightly convene the Elders and inquire into the matter and they shall hear both sides, first alone, then together.

94. And they shall decide justly, not favoring the one side or the other.

95. Ever recognizing there be people who can never agree to work under others.

96. But at the same time, there be some people who cannot rule justly.

97. To those who ever must be chief, there is one answer.

98. Void the Coven, or seek another one or make a Coven of your own, taking with you those who will go.

99. To those who cannot rule justly the answer be, "Those who cannot bear your rule will leave you."

100. For none may come to meetings with those with whom they are at variance.

101. So, an either cannot agree, "Get hence, for the Craft must ever survive."

SO BE IT ARDANE.

102. In the olden days, when we had power, we could use the Art against any who ill-treated the Brotherhood. But in these evil days, we must not do so! For our enemies have devised a burning pit of everlasting fire, into which they say their God casteth all the people who worship Him, except it be the very few who are released by their priest's spells and masses. And this be chiefly by giving monies and rich gifts to receive His favor, for their God is ever in need of money.

103. But as our Gods need our aid to make fertility for man and crops, so it is the God of the Christians ever is in need of man's help to search out and destroy us. Their priests ever tell them that any who get our help are damned to this Hell forever, so men be mad with the terror of it.

104. But they make men believe that they may escape this Hell if they give Witches to the tormentors. So for this reason, all be forever spying, thinking,

"An I catch but one of the Wicca, I will escape this fiery pit."

105. So for this reason we have our hidels, and men searching long and not finding say: "There be none, or if there be, they be in a far country."

106. But when one of our oppressors dies, or even be sick, ever is the cry, "This be Witches' malice," and the hunt is up again, and though they slay ten of their own to one of ours, still they care not. They have countless thousands.

107. While we are few indeed.

SO BE IT ARDANE.

108. That none shall use the Art in any way to do ill to any.

109. However much they injure us, HARM NONE and now times many believe we exist not.

SO BE IT ARDANE.

110. That this Law shall ever continue to help us in our plight. No one, however great an injury or injustice they receive, may use the Art in any way to do ill or harm any. But they may, after great consultations with all, use the Art to restrain Christians from harming us or tax others, but only to let or constrain them.

111. To this end, men will say: "Such an one is a mighty searcher out and a persecutor of old women whom they deemeth to be Witches, and none hath done him skith, so they be proof they cannot, or more truly where be none."

112. For all know full well, that so many folk have died because someone had a grudge against them, or were persecuted because they had money or goods to seize, or because they had none to bribe the searchers. And many have died because they were scolding old women. So much that men now say that "only old women are Witches."

113. And this be to our advantage, and turns suspicions away from us.

114. In England and Scotland, 'tis now many a year since a Witch hath died the death. But misuse of the power might raise the persecution again.

115. So never break this Law, however much you are tempted, and never consent to it being broken in the least.

116. If you know it is being broken, you must work strongly against it.

117. And any High Priestess who consents to its breach must immediately be deposed. "For 'tis the blood of the Brethren they endanger."

118. Do good, and it be safe and only if it be safe.

119. And strictly keep to the old Law.

120. Never accept money for the use of the Art. For money ever smeareth the taker. "'Tis sorcerers and conjurers and priests of the Christians who ever accept money for the use of their Arts. And they sell dwale, and evil loves spells and pardons, so let men escape from their sins."

121. Be not as these. If you accept no money, you will be free from temptation to use the Art for evil causes.

122. All may use the Art for their own advantage, or for the advantage of the Craft, only if you are sure you harm none.

123. But ever let the Coven debate this at length. Only if all be satisfied and none be harmed may the Art be used.

124. If it is not possible to achieve your ends one way, perchance the aim may be achieved by acting in a different way, so as to harm none. May the Curse of the Goddess be on any who breaketh this Law.

SO BE IT ARDANE

125. 'Tis judged lawful an any of the Craft need a house or land and none will sell, to incline the owner's mind so as to be willing to sell, providing it harmeth it not in any way and the full price is paid, without haggling,

126. Never bargain or cheapen anything whilst you live by the Art.

SO BE IT ARDANE.

127. 'Tis the old Law and the most important of all Laws that no one may do anything which will endanger any of the Craft, or bring them into contact with the law of the land, or any of our persecutors.

128. In any disputes between the brethren, no one may invoke any Laws but those of the Craft.

129. Or any tribunal but that of the Priestess, Priest, and Elders. And may the Curse of the Goddess be on any who do so.

SO BE IT ARDANE.

130. It is not forbidden to say as Christians do: "There be Witchcraft in the land," because our oppressors of old make it heresy not to believe in Witchcraft, and so a crime to deny it, which thereby puts you under suspicion.

131. But ever say "I know not of it here, perchance there may be, but afar off—I know not where."

132. But ever speak of those as old crones, consorting with the Devil and riding through the air.

133. But ever say: "But how many men may ride through the air an they be not light as thistledown?"

134. But the Curse of the Goddess be on any who cast any suspicion on any of the Brotherhood.

135. Or who speaks of any real meeting place where any abide.

SO BE IT ARDANE

136. Let the Craft keep books with the names of all herbs which are good for men, and all cures, so all may learn.

137. But keep another book with all the Bales and Apies and let only the Elders and other trustworthy people have this knowledge.

SO BE IT ARDANE.

138. Remember the Art is the secret of the Gods and only may be used in earnest and never for show or pride, or vainglory.

139. Magicians and Christians may taunt us saying, "You have no power. Do magic before our eyes. Then only will we believe." Seeking to cause us to betray our Art before them.

140. Heed them not. For the Art is holy, and may only be used in need. And the Curse of the Gods be on any who break this Law.

SO BE IT ARDANE.

141. It ever be the way with women, and with men also that they ever seek new love.

142. Nor should we reprove them for this.

143. But it may be found to the disadvantage of the Craft.

144. As, so many a time it has happened that a High Priest or High Priestess impelled by love, hath departed with their love; that is, they have left the Coven.

145. Now if a High Priestess wishes to resign, they may do so in full Coven.

146. And this resignation is valid.

147. But if they should run off without resignation, who may know if they may not return within a few months?

148. So the Law is: If a High Priestess leaves her Coven, but returns within the space of a year and a day, then she shall be taken back and all shall be as before.

149. Meanwhile, if she has a deputy, that deputy shall act as High Priestess for as long as the High Priestess is away.

150. If she returns not at the end of a year and a day, then shall the Coven elect a new High Priestess.

151. Unless there be a good reason to the contrary, the person who has done the work should reap the benefit of the reward.

152. If somebody else is elected, the deputy is made maiden and deputy of the High Priestess.

SO BE IT ARDANE.

153. It hath been found that practicing the Art doth cause a fondness between aspirant and tutor, and it is the cause of better results if this be so.

154. But if for any reason this be undesirable, it can easily be avoided by both persons from the outset firmly resolving in their minds that if any such ensue, it shall be that of brother and sister, or parent and child.

155. And it is for this reason that a man may be taught by a woman and a woman by a man and

that woman and woman and man and man
should never attempt these practices together.

156. And may all the Curses of the Mighty Ones be on
any who make such an attempt.

SO BE IT ARDANE.

157. Order and discipline must be kept.

158. A High Priestess or a High Priest may and should
punish all faults.

159. To this end: all the Craft must receive their
correction willingly.

160. All, properly prepared, the culprit kneeling,
should be told his fault, and his sentence
pronounced.

161. Punishment should be the S followed by
something amusing such as several S S S S, or
something of this nature.

162. The culprit must acknowledge the justice of the
punishment by kissing the hand of the Priestess
and by kissing the S on receiving sentence; and
again thanking for punishment received.

SO BE IT ARDANE.

2

THE RITUALS

To Open the Circle

Let all be clean before the Gods. Being properly prepared, purify each other with Scourge or Cord: 3, 7, 9,
21 = 40. Give kiss. High Priest lights two white candles
and places on Altar. Then place a white candle on each
cardinal point of the Magic Circle.

Purify water and salt. First place point of Athame in
water with right hand. Pronounce:

> *I exorcise Thee, O Creature of water, that*
> *though cast out from Thee all the impurities*
> *and uncleanlinesses of the Spirits of*
> *Phantasm. In the names of Arida and*
> *Kernunnos.*

Touching salt with Athame, pronounce:

> *Blessings be upon Thee, O Creature of salt.*
> *Let all malignity and hindrance pass*
> *henceforth and let all good enter in (but ever*
> *are we mindful that as water purifies the*
> *body so the salt purifies the soul). Wherefore*
> *do I bless Thee in the names of Arida and*
> *Kernunnos, that Thou mayest aid me.*

Then transfer three measures of salt with tip of Athame into the water and stir in clockwise direction three times. The Athame is now ready and purified.

Draw a nine-foot Magic Circle (or smaller or larger) as required with Athame, commencing in the East and ending in the East. The circle must be cut in an unbroken line. Then return to Altar facing North.

Take up water with right hand, transfer to left hand. Go to the East and sprinkle (aspurge) with fingers in the East, South, West, and North, finish in the East. Return to Altar.

Take up incense and Censer in right hand. Repeat motions, censing Circle as before. Return to Altar.

The celebrants then anoint the opposite sex with water and salt in the 1, 2, 3, triangle and censes likewise.

Take a bell in right hand. Place in left hand, take Athame in right hand. Go to the East and salute in the following manner: Athame to lips, straight out above eye level, back to lips, then to right side down, with outstretched arm, and back to "carry" position before the right breast.

Cut large clear Pentacle, then pronounce:

> *Hear Ye, O Mighty Ones, Dread Lords of the Watchtowers of the East. I (your name), Priestess and Witch, do summon you, and I do command your presence at this our meeting, that our Circle be guarded and our rites be witnessed.*

Strike bell with Athame once in the East, South, West, and North. Finally giving salute only in the East. All present salute. The Circle is now perfect.

Dance around the Circle. High Priestess leading chanting of the ancient call. Dance and chant. Open Circle with ancient chant:

> *EKO EKO AZARAK,*
> *EKO EKO ZOMELEK,*
> *EKO EKO ARIDA,*
> *EKO EKO KERNUNNOS,*
> *BEZABI, LACHA, BACHABABA.*
> *LAMACH, CAHI, ACHABABA,*
> *KARRELOS, CAHI, ACHABABA,*
> *LAMACH LAMACH BACHAROUS,*
> *CARBAHAJI, SABALYOS,*
> *BARYLOS.*
> *LAZOS, ATHAME, CALYOLAS,*
> *SAMAHAC, ET FAMYOLAS,*
> *HARRAHYA!*

If there is Coven Work to be done, now is the proper time to do it. To close or dismiss the Magic Circle. High Priestess/Priest, with ATHAME, goes to the East, salute; Then all present salute. Then celebrant or High Priestess says:

> *Hear Ye, O Mighty Ones. We thank you for*
> *your attendance, and 'ere Ye depart to your*
> *lovely realms, we bid you Hail and Farewell.*

All present repeat *"Hail and Farewell"* and point Athames high. Repeat at other quarters, South, West, North, and finishing in the East. Give final salute.

Initiation of the First Degree

The Circle is cast in the usual manner. All except High Priestess, High Priest, and Handmaiden will leave the Circle. The initiate having been ritually washed and blindfolded, is led in naked.

High Priestess or High Priest takes Athame or Sword and cuts doorway perfectly in Northeast and places tip of weapon at heart of postulant and says:

> O thou who standeth on the threshold of pleant, world of men, and the domains of the Dread Lords of the outer spaces, hast Thou the courage to make the essay?

Postulant:

> I have.

High Priestess:

> For I say verily, it were better to rush upon my weapon and perish than to make the attempt with fear in thy heart.

Postulant:

> I have two passwords.

High Priestess:

> What are the two passwords?

Postulant:

> Perfect love and perfect peace.

High Priestess: (Drops weapon and says)

*All who bring such words are doubly
welcome.*

High Priestess: (She closes Circle and places weapon on Altar, goes behind postulant. Puts left arm around waist, pulls postulant's head around over right shoulder, with right arm, and kisses lips and says:) *I give you a third password—a kiss.* (High Priestess pushes postulant into Circle with her body and releasing postulant says:)

*This is the way all are first brought into the
Circle.*

She then leads Postulant sunwise to the South of the Altar and says:

*O Thou who hast declared intent to become
one of us, hear then that which thou must
know to do. Single is the race, single of men
and of Gods, from a single source we both
draw breath, but a difference of power in
everything keeps us apart, for we are as
nothing, but the Gods stay forever. Yet we
can, in greatness of minds, be like the Gods.
Though we know not to what goal by day or
in the night. Fate has written that we shall
run beyond all seas, and earth's last
boundaries, beyond the Spring of night and
the Heavens' vast expanse there lies a majesty
which is the domain of the Gods. Those who
would pass through the Gates of Night and
Day to that sweet place, which is between the
world of men and the domains of the Lords of*

the outer spaces. *Know that unless there is truth in thy heart, thy every effort is doomed to failure. HEAR THEN THE LAW. That Thou lovest all things in nature. That thou shalt suffer no person to be harmed by thy hands or in thy mind. That thou walkest humbly in the ways of men and the ways of the Gods. Also it is the Law that contentment thou shalt learn, through suffering, and from long years and from nobility of mind and of purpose. FOR THE WISE NEVER GROW OLD. Their minds are nourished by living in the daylight of the Gods and if among the vulgar some discoveries should arise concerning some maxims of thy belief in the Gods, so do thou, for the most part, keep silent. For there is a great risk that thou straightway vomit up that which thou hast not digested and when someone shall say to thee, thou knowest naught and it bites thee not, then knowest thou that thou hast begun the work, and as sheep do not bring their food to the Shepherd to show how much they have eaten, but digesting inwardly their provender, bear outwardly wool and milk. Even so, do not thou display the maxims to the vulgar, but rather the works that flow when they are digested. Now there is the ordeal.*

High Priestess takes stout Cord, ties Cord around postulant's right ankle leaving ends free, and says:

Feet neither bound nor free.

High Priestess takes longer Cord and ties wrists behind back, then bringing Cord around neck and tying in the front. Taking Cord in the left hand with Athame in right, leads postulant sunwise and pointing Athame high with arm outstretched, says:

Take heed O Lords of the Watchtowers of the East that (initiate) *properly prepared will be made Priest/Priestess and Witch.*

She repeats this at the South, West, North, returning to the East salutes, returning with postulant to South of the Altar, Clasping postulant around body with left arm, runs Deosil three times around the Altar.

High Priestess says to Postulant: *Kneel.*

High Priestess strikes eleven strokes on the bell and says to postulant:

Rise. In other religions the postulant kneels as the Priest claims supreme power, but in the Art Magical, we are taught to be humble, and we kneel and we say: Blessed are thy feet, that have brought thee in thy ways. (kiss feet)*; Blessed be thy knees, that shall kneel at the sacred Altar.* (kiss knees)*; Blessed be thy groins* (womb if female) *without which we would not be.* (kiss groins)*; Blessed be thy breasts* (if female)*, erected in beauty and in*

strength. (kiss breasts)*; Blessed be thy lips,*
which shall utter the sacred names. (kiss lips).

Take measure with a reel of white cotton:
  Around Head—tie a knot.
  Around Breast—tie a knot.
  Around Hips—tie a knot.
  The Height—tie a knot.

Then break cotton and roll up around the finger. With needle or pin, prick thumb, catching blood on measure. Place measure on Altar. Make postulant kneel. Tie both feet together with Cord already around the ankles. Then attach Cord to the Altar. Strike bell three times with Athame and say:

High Priestess:

> *Art ready to swear thou wilt always be true to*
> *the art?*

Postulant:

> *Yes.*

High Priestess strikes seven times on bell with Athame and says:

> *Thou must first be purified.*

Take Scourge and strike postulant's bottom 3, 7, 9, 21 times (40 times in all) then High Priestess says:

> *Art always ready to protect, help, and defend*
> *thy Brothers and Sisters of the Art?*

Postulant:

> *Yes.*

High Priestess:

> *Then say after me: I* (postulant's name), *in
> the presence of the Mighty Ones, do of my
> own free will and accord, most solemnly
> swear, without any reservation in me
> whatsoever, that I will ever keep secret and
> never reveal the secrets of the Arts, except it
> be to a person properly prepared, within such
> a Circle as I am now in, and that I will never
> deny the secrets to such a person if they be
> properly vouched for by a Brother or Sister of
> the Art. All this do I swear by my hopes of a
> future life. Mindful that, my measure has
> been taken, and may my weapons turn
> against me if I break this my solemn oath.*

Loosen Cords from ankles, then Cord from Altar, leaving hands bound. Remove blindfold, then assist postulant in rising up.

High Priestess:

> *I hereby consecrate thee with oil.* (Making
> sign with oil of the First Degree) *I hereby
> consecrate thee with wine.* (Making sign
> with wine of the First Degree) *I hereby
> consecrate thee with water.* (Making sign
> of the First Degree with water.) *I hereby
> consecrate thee with fire.* (Making sign with
> incense of First Degree.) *I hereby consecrate
> thee with my lips, Priest* (or Priestess) *and
> Witch.* (Making sign of the First Degree
> with a kiss.)

She unties hands and says:

Now I present you with the working tools of the Witch. First, the Magic Sword, with this and with the Athame, thou canst form all Magic Circles. Subdue and punish all rebellious Spirits and Demons, and even persuade the evil Genii. With this in your hand, Thou art ruler of the Magic Circle. (kiss) *Next I present the Athame. This is the true Witches' weapon and it has all the powers of the Magic Sword.* (kiss) *Next I present the white-handled Knife. Its use is to form all instruments used in the Art. It can only be used within a Magic Circle.* (kiss) *Next I present the Magic Wand. Its use is to control properly certain Genii to whom it would not be mete to use the Magic Sword or Athame.* (kiss) *Next I present the Pentacle. This is for the purpose of calling up the appropriate Spirits.* (kiss) *Next I present the Censer of incense. This is used to encourage and welcome good Spirits and to banish evil Spirits.* (kiss) *Next I present the Scourge. This is a sign of power and domination. It is also used to cause suffering and purification. For it is written, "To learn thou must suffer and be purified." Art thou willing to suffer to learn?*

Postulant:

I am. (kiss)

56 / The Rituals

High Priestess:

> *Next and lastly, I present the Cords. They are*
> *of use to bind the Sigils of the Art—the*
> *material basis. Also they are necessary in the*
> *oath and to enforce thy will* (kiss). *I now*
> *salute you in the names of Arida and*
> *Kernunnos newly made Priest/Priestess*
> *and Witch.*

High Priestess then leads postulant to the East. Salutes with Athame and proclaims:

> *Hear Ye, O Mighty Ones.* (Name of witch)
> *has been consecrated a Priest/High Priestess*
> *of the Art and a Brother/Sister of the Wicca.*

This is repeated at the South, West, North, and finishing with salute at the East then returns to the Altar.

The Quaich (drinking horn, glass, or cup) is filled with wine. Others present then enter the Circle through the doorway cut by High Priestess or High Priest. New Witch is presented to Coven members. The Quaich is passed around the Circle, where all drink, then give it back to the High Priestess, who drains it. Postulant can be asked to relate any psychic experiences and can be shown the circle dance. Finish with *Cakes and Wine ceremony* which will follow, and a feast in Circle before closing (or after closing Circle). Feasting and dancing are permitted in Circle but I feel this should be done after closing the working Circle.

Elevation to the Second Degree

Form a circle. The Initiate must be properly prepared and bound. All are purified including the Initiate. High Priestess/High Priest proclaims at the four quarters.

High Priestess:

> *Hear ye, Ye Mighty Ones.* (Initiate's witch name), *a duly consecrated Priestess/Priest and Witch is now properly prepared to be elevated to the Second Degree.*

High Priestess circles with Initiate three times with dance step. Initiate now kneels at the Altar and is secured at hands and feet. High Priestess/High Priest says:

> *To attain this degree it is necessary to be purified. Art willing to suffer to learn?*

Initiate: *I am.*

High Priestess/High Priest says:

> *I purify thee to take this oath rightly.*

High Priestess strikes three on the bell. Scourges 3, 7, 9, 21 then says:

> *Repeat after me: I,* (initiate's witch name), *swear on my Mother's womb, and by my honor amongst men, and by my Brothers and Sisters of the Art, that I will never reveal any secrets of the Art, except it be to a worthy person properly prepared in the center of a*

*Magic Circle, such as I am now in. This I
swear by my past lives and by my hopes of future ones to come and I devote myself to utter
destruction if I break this my solemn oath.*

High Priestess/High Priest kneels, places left hand
under Initiate's knees and right hand on his/her head
and says:

I will all my power into thee.

Loosens Cords from Altar and ankles and assists
Initiate to rise. The consecration now follows.

High Priestess/High Priest makes the Pentagram on
the genitals, right foot, left knee, right knee, left foot,
genitals, and says:

I consecrate Thee with oil (kiss).
I consecrate Thee with Wine (kiss).
I consecrate Thee with Water (kiss).
1 consecrate Thee with fire (kiss).
I consecrate Thee with my lips (kiss).

Unbind hands, then present tools to Initiate.

High Priestess/High Priest:

*You will now use the tools in turn. First the
Magic Sword—redraw the Magic Circle.*

Initiate does this, then hands back tool to High
Priest who gives it a kiss.

High Priestess:

*Second, the Athame—redraw the Magic
Circle.*

Initiate does this, then hands back tool to High Priestess who gives it a kiss.

High Priestess:

> *Third, the White-handled Knife—inscribe a Pentagram on a candle.*

Initiate does this, then hands back tool to High Priestess who gives it a kiss.

High Priestess:

> *Fourth, the Wand—wave to the Four Quarters.*

Initiate does this, then hands back tool to High Priestess who it a kiss.

High Priestess:

> *Fifth, the Pentacle—show to the Four Quarters.*

Initiate does this, then hands back tool to High Priestess who gives it a kiss.

High Priestess:

> *Sixth, the Censer—cense the Circle.*

Initiate does this, then hands back tool to High Priestess who gives it a kiss.

High Priestess:

> *Seventh, the Cords—bind the High Priestess/ High Priest.*

Initiate does this and High Priestess/High Priest gives a kiss.

High Priestess says:

> *Learn that in Witchcraft thou must ever*
> *return triple. As I scourge thee, thou must*
> *scourge me, but triple. Where I gave thee*
> *three strokes, return nine; seven strokes,*
> *return twenty-one; nine strokes, return*
> *twenty-seven; twenty-one strokes, return*
> *sixty-three. That is 120 strokes in all. Take*
> *up the Scourge.*

Initiate does so and purifies the High Priestess with 120 strokes, then unbinds High Priestess/High Priest who gives a kiss. High Priestess/High Priest then says:

> *Thou hast obeyed the Law but mark well,*
> *when thou receiveth good, so equally art thou*
> *bound to return good threefold.*

The Initiate is then presented to the Four Quarters.

High Priestess/High Priest says:

> *Hail Ye, Mighty Ones, take heed that* (name
> of initiate) *hath been duly raised to the*
> *Second Degree.*

Finally salute East as usual. Return to center and finish. [Note: Only Second Degree Witches should attend at this stage of elevation.]

Initiation of the Third Degree

High Priest, High Priestess, and Third Degree witches only attend. In the absence of sufficient Initiates, use the people who are being instructed to enact after describing the Saga.

The High Priestess and High Priest are doubly purified. Others purified in usual manner. Circle is opened in the usual way. Initiates sit in cross-legged position around the Circle. Magus or High Priestess then says:

Having learned thus far, you must know why the Wicca are called "The Hidden Children of the Goddess."

Then the Legend of the Goddess is narrated or enacted by High Priestess and High Priest. The High Priestess takes off her necklace and lays it on the Altar. She then puts on a veil and jewelry. The High Priest who is taking the part of the God is invested with a Horned Crown and girds on a Sword which he draws and stands in the God position with a Sword and a Scourge by the Altar. High Priestess meantime has left the Circle and stands outside in veil, etc.

The narrator, who must be a Third-Degree witch or one of the Initiates, says:

In Ancient time, Our Lord, The Great Horned One, was as He still is, The Consoler, The Comforter, but men knew him as the Dread Lord of the Shadows—lonely—stern and just, but Our Lady, The Goddess, would solve all mysteries—even the mystery of

Death. And so She journeyed to the
Netherlands, The Guardian of the Portal
challenged her.

The High Priestess taking the part of the Goddess advances to the Side of the Magic Circle. The Guardian (whoever is taking the part of the Guardian, and it can be the Narrator) challenges her with the Sword or Athame.

Guardian of the Portal says:

Strip off thy garments, lay aside thy jewels,
for naught may ye bring with thee into this
our land.

Narrator:

So she laid down her garments and her jewels
and was bound as all living must be who seek
to enter the realms of Death, The Mighty
Ones.

The High Priestess takes off the veil and jewelry, and lays them down outside the Circle. The Guardian of the Portal binds her with Cords and brings her inside the Circle.

Narrator:

Such was her beauty that Death himself knelt
and laid his Sword and Crown at her feet
and kissed her feet.

The High Priest comes forward and gazes at her, and He lays the Horned Crown and the Sword at the feet of the High Priestess and kisses her feet. High Priest and High Priestess repeat words after spoken by narrator.

Narrator:

Blessed are thy feet that have brought thee in these ways. Abide with me, but let me place my cold hand on thy heart. (High Priest repeats.)

Narrator:

And she replied, "I love thee not." (High Priestess repeats.)

Narrator:

Why dost thou cause all things that I love and take delight in, to fade and die?" (High Priestess repeats.)

Narrator:

"Lady, " replied Death, "'Tis age and fate, against which I am helpless. Age causes all things to wither, but when men die, at the end of time, I give them rest and strength so that they may return. But you, you are lovely. Return not: abide with me." (High Priest repeats.)

Narrator:

But she answers, "I love thee not." (High Priestess repeats.)

Narrator:

> "Then," said Death, "An you receive not my
> hand on your heart, you must kneel at
> Death's Scourge."

(High Priest repeats, then he rises and takes up the Scourge from the Altar.)

Narrator:

> "It is fate, better so," she replied. (High
> Priestess repeats.) And she knelt.

The High Priestess kneels before the Altar and the High Priest uses the Scourge 3, 7, 9, 21 = 40 times.

Narrator:

> And Death scourged her tenderly, and she
> cried, "I knew the pangs of love." (High
> Priestess repeats.)

Narrator:

> And Death raised her and said, "Blessed Be."
> And gave her the fivefold kiss saying, "Thus
> only may you attain to joy and knowledge."

(High Priest repeats, and then raises the High Priestess and gives her the fivefold kiss and unfastens her cords.)

Narrator:

> And he taught her all the mysteries, and he
> gave her the necklace which is the circle of
> rebirth.

High Priest takes High Priestess' necklace from the Altar and replaces it about her neck. The High Priestess takes up the Sword and Horned Crown from the floor where the High Priest placed them, and gives them back to him. Then he stands as before, by the Altar, in the position of the God and she stands by his side in the Pentacle position of the Goddess.

Narrator:

And she taught him the mystery of the sacred cup which is the cauldron of rebirth. They loved and were one, for there be three great mysteries in the life of man. Magic (love) controls them all. For to fulfill love, you must return again at the same time, and at the same place, as the loved one, and you must meet, and know and remember and love them again. But to be reborn, you must die, and be made ready for a new body, and to die you must be born, and without love, you may not be born. And our Goddess ever inclineth to love and mirth and happiness and guardeth and cherisheth Her hidden children in life: And in death She teacheth the way to have communion, and even in the world, She teacheth them the Mystery of the Magic Circle, which is placed between the worlds.

The High Priestess and High Priest then replace the Scourge, and the Sword, Crown and etc. upon the Altar. The High Priestess and High Priest then invite

the Initiates to ask questions on the Legend of the Goddess, which must be answered truthfully and also explain the symbolism contained in the Legend including the Great Rite. Cakes and wine follow.

The Circle is closed.

The Great Rite

In ancient times the Great Rite was practiced, but I do not know of any Witches in America or England who still practice the Great Rite. You may reject it, or if you feel closer to the Gods by returning as much as possible to the worship of the Ancients, then by all means do it.

THE GREAT RITE—at the end of each Sabbat Rite, the ancient ones had to "Earth" the power that had been raised within the Circle so that the power raised would not remain in the atmosphere afterwards. They earthed the power by committing the "Sex Act," which brought them down from the mystical to the material level. Each Sabbat Rite ended with this act and it was called "The Great Rite."

The Great Rite is performed as an act of worship to the God and Goddess. Obviously, if everybody indulged in lovemaking at the end of the rite, within the Magic Circle, it would look as if an orgy were taking place. Mostly the coveners did this in private after leaving the Magic Circle. Sex Magic is one of the most powerful of all acts of Magic and not to be taken lightly and certainly I believe should be performed in private before the Gods.

The Charge of the Goddess

Listen to the words of the Great Mother, who was of old, called amongst men, Artemis, Astarte, Dione, Melusine, Aphrodite, Cerridwen, Diana, Arionhod, Bride, and by many other names.

> *At mine Altar, the youths of Lacedemon in Sparta made due sacrifice. Whenever ye have need of anything, once in the month and better it be when the Moon is Full, then shall ye assemble in some secret place and adore the Spirit of Me, who am Queen of all the Witcheries. There shall Ye assemble, who are feign to learn all sorceries who have not as yet won my deepest secrets. To these will I teach that which is is yet unknown. And ye shall be free from all slavery and as a sign that ye be really free, ye shall be naked in your rites and ye shall sing, feast, make music and love, all in my presence. For mine is the ecstasy of the Spirit and mine is also joy on earth. For my Law is love unto all beings. Keep pure your highest ideals, strive ever towards them. Let none stop you or turn you aside. For mine is the secret that opens upon the door of youth and mine is the Cup of the Wine of Life and the Cauldron of Cerridwen, which is the Holy Grail of Immortality. I am the Gracious Goddess who gives the gift of joy unto the heart of man upon earth. I give the*

*knowledge of the Spirit Eternal, and beyond
death I give peace and freedom and reunion
with those that have gone before. Nor do I
demand aught or sacrifice, for behold I am
the Mother of all things, and my love
is poured out upon the earth.*

Hear ye the words of the Star Goddess. She, in the dust of whose feet are the Hosts of Heaven, whose body encircleth the universe.

*I who am the beauty of the Green Earth, and
the White Moon amongst the stars and the
mystery of the Waters, and the desire of the
heart of man, I call unto thy soul to arise and
come unto me. For I am the Soul of Nature
who giveth life to the universe; from me all
things proceed and unto me all things must
return. Beloved of the Gods and men, whose
innermost divine self shall be enfolded in the
raptures of the Infinite, let my worship be in
the heart. Rejoiceth, for behold, all acts of
love and pleasure are my rituals; therefore,
let there be beauty and strength—power and
compassion—honor and humility, mirth and
reverence—within you. And thou who think-
est to seek me, know that thy seeking and
yearning avail thee not unless thou knowest
the mystery, that if that which thou seekest
thou findeth not within thyself, thou wilt
never find it without thee. For behold—*

*I have been with thee from the beginning,
and I am that which is attained at the end
of desire.*

Invocation to the Horned God

By the flame that burneth bright,
O Horned One!
We call Thy name into the night,
O Ancient One!
Thee we invoke, by the Moon-led sea,
By the standing stone and the twisted tree.
Thee we invoke, where gather Thine own,
By the nameless shore, forgotten and lone.
Come where the round of the dance is trod,
Horn and Hoof of the Goat Foot God!
By moonlit meadow, on dusky hill,
When the haunted wood is hushed and still,
Come to the charm of the chanted prayer,
As the Moon bewitches the midnight air.
Evoke Thy powers that potent bide,
In shining stream and the secret tide.
In fiery flame by starlight pale,
In shadowy host that rides the gale.
And by the ferndrakes, fairy haunted,
Of forests wild and woods enchanted,
Come? O Come!
To the Heart-beat's drum!
Come to us who gather below,
When the broad white Moon is climbing slow.
Through the stars to the heavens' height,
We hear Thy hoofs on the wind of night!
As black tree branches shake and sigh,

By joy and terror we know Thee nigh.
We speak the spell Thy power unlocks,
At Solstice, Sabbat, and Equinox!

Ceremony of the Blessing of Cakes and Wine

High Priestess stands in the God position. Feet are together, arms crossed under breasts, the Athame in right hand, the Scourge in the left hand. High Priest kisses her feet, then knees, then kneels with head below High Priestess' knees and adores.

High Priest fills Quaich and offers to the High Priestess who, holding Athame between the palms, places the point in the cup and says:

High Priestess:

As the Athame is the male, so the Cup is the
female and enjoined they bring happiness.

High Priestess lays Athame aside and drinks from Cup and passes to all coveners. Each drinks. The Cup returns to the High Priestess, Who drains the Cup. High Priest presents cakes on Pentacle to the High Priestess who blesses with Athame. High Priest lifts cakes on Pentacle and says:

Oh Queen, most secret, Bless this food unto
our bodies, bestowing wealth, strength, joy,
and peace, and that fulfillment of love which
is perpetual happiness.

The High Priest again presents the cakes to the High Priestess, Who eats while the High Priest again offers Her the Cup. All present sit and the High Priest invites the High Priestess to join them. The Paten of cakes and the Cup of Wine is passed to all present.

Witches' Chant

Darksome night and shining Moon,
Hearken to the Witches' rune.
East then South, West then North,
Hear! Come! I call Thee forth!

By all the powers of land and sea,
Be obedient unto me.
Wand and Pentacle and Sword,
Hearken ye unto my word.

Cords and Censer, Scourge and Knife,
Waken all ye into life.
Powers of the Witches' Blade,
Come ye as the charge is made.

Queen of Heaven, Queen of Hell,
Send your aid unto the spell.
Horned Hunter of the night,
Work my will by magic rite.

By all the powers of land and sea,
As I do say, "So mote it be."
By all the might of Moon and Sun,
As I do will, it shall be done.

Incantation

ENOS, ARIDA JUVATE
ENOS, ARIDA JUVATE
ENOS, ARIDA JUVATE
NEVE, LUERVE, KERNUNNOS
NEVE, LUERVE, KERNUNNOS
NEVE, LUERVE, KERNUNNOS
SINS INCURRERE IN PLEORES
SINS INCURRERE IN PLEORES
SINS INCURRERE IN PLEORES
SATUR FU FERE DIANUS
SATUR FU FERE DIANUS
SATUR FU FERE DIANUS
LINEN SALI STA BERBER
LINEN SALI STA BERBER
LINEN SALI STA BERBER
TRIUMPHE
TRIUMPHE
TRIUMPHE
SEMUNIS ALTERNIE ADVOCAPITO
SEMUNIS ALTERNIE ADVOCAPITO
SEMUNIS ALTERNIE ADVOCAPITO
CONCTOS
CONCTOS
CONCTOS

Drawing Down the Moon

This ceremony can be performed when holding Esbats at Full Moon or when Moon is waxing. High Priestess or High Priest casts the Circle. Coveners are properly prepared and purified. High Priestess assumes Goddess position.

High Priest draws down the Moon on either High Priestess or Handmaiden. A period of silence usually follows for many things may happen when this is done for it is a very powerful ceremony.

The High Priest will stand before the High Priestess, who is in the Osiris or God Position, and the High Priest will say:

> *I invoke Thee and call upon Thee, O Mighty*
> *Mother of us all. Bringer of Fruitfulness by*
> *seed and by root. I invoke Thee, by stem and*
> *by bud. I invoke Thee, by life and by love and*
> *call upon Thee to descend into the body of*
> *this Thy Priestess and Servant. Hear with her*
> *ears, speak with her tongue, touch with her*
> *hands, kiss with her lips, that thy servants*
> *may be fulfilled.*

The High Priestess then adopts the Goddess position and the High Priest draws down the power by the force of his concentration and prayer, touching her on the breast and womb with the Wand. He then kneels at her feet and adores while concentrating. The High Priestess shall then recite The Charge.

> *All ye assembled at mine shrine,*
> *Mother Darksome and Divine.*

Mine the Scourge and mine the Kiss,
Here I charge you in this sign.

(Assumes God position.)

All ye assembled in my sight,
Bow before my spirit bright.

(Coveners bow before High Priestess.)

Aphrodite, Arionhod,
Lover of the Horned God,
Mighty Queen of Witchery and night,
Morgan, Etoine, Nisene,
Diana, Bridgid, Melusine,
Am I named of old by men,
Artemis and Cerridwen,
Hell's dark mistress, Heaven's queen.
Ye who would ask of me a rune,
Or who would ask of me a boon,
Meet me in some secret glade
Dance my round in greenwood shade,
By the light of the Full Moon.
In a place, wild and lone,
Dance about mine altar stone;
Work my holy mystery.
Ye who are feign to sorcery,
I bring ye secrets yet unknown.
No more shall ye know slavery,
Who give true worship unto me.
Ye who tread my round on Sabbat night,
Come ye all naked to the rite,

In token that ye be really free.
I teach ye the mystery of rebirth,
Work ye my mysteries in mirth.
Heart joined to heart and lip to lip,
Five are the points of fellowship,
That bring ye ecstasy on earth,
For I am the circle of rebirth.
I ask no sacrifice, but do bow,
No other Law but love I know,
By naught but love may I be known.
All things living are mine own,
From me they come, to me they go.

Close and dismiss Circle.

Ancient Wiccan Grace

Answer us, O Ancient Horned One,
Provender and power are Thine.
Hear and answer, Gracious Goddess,
Grant us laughter, wit and wine,
Descend on us, O Thou of blessings,
Come among us, make us glad.
Since Thou art Chief of our creation,
Why, O Why should we be sad?
Beam on us, O joyous Bacchus,
Banish heavy-hearted hate.
Accept our Craft, O Greatest Mother,
Let cheerful brightness be our fate.
SO MOTE IT BE!

Ancient Runic Spell

Upon this Candle I will write,
What I receive of Thee this night.
Grant what I wish You to do,
I dedicate this Rite to You.
I trust that You will grant this Boon,
O Lovely Goddess, of the Moon.

I call Earth to bond my Spell
Air speed its travel well,
Fire give It Spirit from Above,
Water quench my Spell with Love.

To Consecrate All Your Ritual Instruments

High Priest or High Priestess casts the Magic Circle. All attending must be properly prepared and purified. High Priest or High Priestess faces the Altar in North. Coveners form circle and each holds in his strongest hand the tools he is consecrating. High Priest or High Priestess anoints all ritual instruments being held by coveners.

High Priest or High Priestess invokes the Watchers to bear witness as the instruments are consecrated to the Craft.

High Priestess:

> *Coveners! In your words and by the force of your will power and imagination, charge your* (name of tool) *concentrating on the purpose you wish the* (name of tool) *to serve.*
>
> *Grasp the* (name of tool) *in your strongest hand and concentrate your will power into the* (name of tool).
>
> *Concentrate your desire into the* (tool), *that its power will increase with each new day. That its* (name of tool) *power will last as long as the* (tool) *itself. That Ghosts, Spirits, human beings, and animals are to obey your will. That they will obey your magic* (name the tool) *whether in the*

*physical world or on the Astral (spiritual) or
Mental plane.*

Charge your (name the tool) *to work on
dead material also.*

Concentrate on the Universal God Force
(Akasha principle) *and draw down this Life
Force from the Great Universal God Force
into your* (tool).

Charge your (name the tool) *with the
knowledge that the Life Force Power in the*
(tool) *will automatically intensify from one
day to the next.*

Charge your (tool) *to automatically,
without any effort on your part, bring a piece
of Life Force from the Universal Life Force,
which will then radiate from your* (tool)
whenever and to whatever it is needed.

This force or power in your (name of
tool) *can be used for the good of yourself and
for others as you wish, or if necessary it may
be used against your enemies.*

SO MOTE IT BE.

3

THE SABBATS

Our belief that the Moon being a physical manifestation of the power and glory of the Goddess, the Sabbat Rites are celebrated at midnight on the night before the day of the festival.

We have eight Great Sabbat Festivals and thirteen New Moon and thirteen Full Moon Esbats during the year. Our religious year begins with Yule. The Great Sabbats are:

> *Yule: December 21. The Winter Solstice. We celebrate the return or rebirth of the Sun.*
>
> *Candlemas: February 2. A fire festival. In olden times all new Witches were initiated at Candlemas, the "Feast of the Waxing Light."*
>
> *The Spring Rite: March 21. The Spring Equinox. The Celebration for fertility of man, crops, and animals.*
>
> *Rudemas: May 1. A fertility Sabbat.*
>
> *Beltane: June 21. Midsummer festival celebrating the Summer Solstice. Gather as many covens together as possible.*

Lammas: August 1. Rites for increase in material supply.

Autumn Equinox Rite: September 21. A celebration of Thanksgiving for the blessings of the year, for food, clothing, and shelter.

Hallowmas: October 31. Celebration for the reunion of Souls of the family members who have left the physical plane. We can ask them to return on this night and give us messages of Wisdom.

I would have you remember that "there is a time and place for all things." Work out your own timetable, according to the phases of the Moon and the movement of the planets for the workings of the Craft. Remember the two sides (light and dark) of the Moon for casting spells. Be sure you have sufficient knowledge of Astrology because if you do not heed the Moon's phases and the elemental power tides, your spell casting will avail you nothing.

It is to your benefit that you celebrate each Great Sabbat and the New Moon and Full Moon Esbats.

The Great Sabbats you are commanded to keep if you would retain your Witch power.

SO BE IT!

The Yule Sabbat

The Celebration of the Rebirth of the Sun

December 21

Let all be properly prepared and purified. High Priest casts the Magic Circle and invokes the Ancient Ones to bear witness. High Priest decorates the Altar (standing in the North of the Circle) with pine boughs, holly, ivy, and mistletoe. Two red candles, incense, oil, and the Sacred Tools of the Craft. A red candle is on the Altar for each covener present.

High Priest places the Cauldron of Keridwen in the center of the Magic Circle and encircles it with a wreath of pine boughs, holly, ivy, and mistletoe. High Priest lays the Balefire within the Cauldron with nine woods: rowan, apple, elder, holly, pine, cedar, juniper, poplar, and dogwood.

High Priestess stands in the West of the Magic Circle facing East and recites:

> *All ye assembled at mine shrine,*
> *Mother Darksome and Divine.*
> *Mine the Scourge and mine the Kiss*
> *Here I charge you in this sign.*

High Priestess assumes the Goddess position.

> *All ye assembled in my sight,*
> *Bow before my spirit bright.*

All coveners bow to High Priestess.

Aphrodite, Arionhod,
Lover of the Horned God,
Mighty Queen of Witchery and night,
Morgan, Etoine, Nisene,
Diana, Bridgid, Melusine,
Am I named of old by men,
Artemis and Cerridwen,
Hell's dark mistress, Heaven's queen.
Ye who would ask of me a rune,
Or who would ask of me a boon,
Meet me in some secret glade,
Dance my round in greenwood shade,
By the light of the Full Moon.
In a place, wild and lone,
Dance about mine altar stone;
Work my holy mystery.
Ye who are feign to sorcery,
I bring ye secrets yet unknown.
No more shall ye know slavery,
Who give true worship unto me.
Ye who tread my round on Sabbat night,
Come Ye all naked to the rite,
In token that ye be really free.
I teach ye the mystery of rebirth,
Work ye my mysteries in mirth.
Heart joined to heart and lip to lip,
Five are the points of fellowship,
That bring ye ecstasy on earth,
For I am the circle of rebirth.

I ask no sacrifice, but do bow,
No other Law but love I know,
By naught but love may I be known.
All things living are mine own,
From me they come, to me they go.

The coveners have remained silent and standing inside the Magic Circle. High Priest kindles the fire of Keridwen by drawing down a spark of elemental fire from the Universal Source. High Priest passes to the East and bows. He returns to the Altar. High Priest assumes the Horned God position and recites Invocation:

By the flame that burneth bright,
O Horned One!
We call Thy name into the night,
O Ancient One
Thee we invoke, by the Moon-led sea,
By the standing stone and the twisted tree.
Thee we invoke, where gather Thine own,
By the nameless shore, forgotten and lone.
Come where the round of the dance is trod,
Horn and Hoof of the Goat Foot God!
By moon lit meadow, on dusky hill,
When the haunted wood is hushed and still,
Come to the charm of the chanted prayer,
As the Moon bewitches the midnight air.
Evoke Thy powers that potent bide,
In shining stream and the secret tide.
In fiery flame by starlight pale,
In shadowy host that rides the gale.

And by the ferndrakes, fairy haunted,
Of forests wild and woods enchanted,
Come? O Come!
To the heart-beat's drum!
Come to us who gather below,
When the broad white Moon is climbing slow.
Through the stars to the heavens' height,
We hear Thy hoofs on the wind of night!
As black tree branches shake and sigh,
By joy and terror we know Thee nigh.
We speak the spell Thy power unlocks,
At Solstice, Sabbat, and Equinox!

The coveners file past, male then female, as they pass the High Priestess, the females curtsy and the males bow and kiss the right cheek of the High Priestess. As they pass the High Priest, he hands each one a red unlit taper from the Altar which they light at the Cauldron and again form a circle line alternately male-female.

High Priestess:

Queen of the Moon,
Queen of the Stars,
Queen of the Horns,
Queen of the Fires,
Queen of the Earth,
Bring to us the Child of Promise!
For it is the Great Mother
Who gives birth to Him;

It is the Lord of Life
Who is born again.
Darkness and tears are set aside,
When the Sun comes up again.
Golden Sun of hill and mountain,
Illumine the world,
Illumine the seas,
Illumine the rivers,
Illumine us all.
Grief be laid and joy be raised,
Blessed be the Great Mother!
Without beginning, without end,
Everlasting to Eternity.
Evoe! Io! Evoe! He!

At this point all raise their lighted tapers high and chant:

Evoe! Io! Evoe! He!
Blessed Be, Blessed Be.

High Priest leads the coveners in a dance around the High Priestess and the Altar chanting.

High Priest:

EKO EKO AZARAK,
EKO EKO ZOMELEK,
EKO EKO ARIDA,
EKO EKO KERNUNNOS,
BEZABI, LACHA, BACHABABA.
LAMACH, CAHI, ACHABABA,
KARRELOS, CAHI, ACHABABA,

LAMACH LAMACH BACHAROUS,
CARBAHAJI, SABALYOS,
BARYLOS.
LAZOS, ATHAME, CALYOLAS,
SAMAHAC, ET FAMYOLAS,
HARRAHYA!

When the HARRAHYA! is chanted the High Priest takes the High Priestess by the hand and leaps the Cauldron. Then each male takes a female by the hand and leaps over the Cauldron. He leaps and holds her hand while she leaps the Cauldron. As each leap is enacted, everyone shouts *"HARRAHYA!"*

High Priestess resumes the Goddess position. High Priest leads the coveners in a file past the High Priestess. As the High Priest passes the High Priestess, he bows and kisses her cheek then resumes his position at Altar, facing East. Places lighted taper on the Altar in a holder provided for this purpose.

As the coveners pass the High Priestess, the females curtsy, the men bow to High Priestess and kiss her on the right cheek. (Kiss of fealty.) As the coveners pass the High Priest, they hand him their lighted tapers which are placed on the Altar.

High Priestess holds the Chalice while the High Priest pours wine into the Chalice. She continues to hold the Chalice over the Cauldron of Keridwen as the High Priest picks up his Athame and plunges it into the Chalice of wine. High Priestess sips from the Chalice and passes the Chalice to the High Priest. He sips the wine and passes the Chalice to the coveners who in turn sip from the Chalice. The cup returns to the High

Priestess (completing the circle) who drains the wine. The High Priestess always finishes the wine in the cup.

High Priest and High Priestess and all coveners face North, East, South, and West and salute with Athames while the High Priest thanks the Ancient Ones and gives them license to depart the Circle.

Celebrate with cakes and wine and much feasting, dancing, and Brotherhood.

The Candlemas Sabbat

The Feast of the Waxing Light

February 2

Let all be properly prepared and purified. High Priest casts the Magic Circle and invokes the Ancient Ones. Altar is placed in the North of Circle and decorated with a wreath of white flowers. Two white altar candles and a white candle for each covener and the Sacred Altar tools. Cauldron placed in the center of the Circle contains the nine woods: rowan, apple, elder, holly, pine, cedar, juniper, poplar, and dogwood.

High Priest stands at Altar facing East. High Priestess enters Circle and stands in the West facing East. The coveners file into the Circle, male and female, and as they pass before the High Priestess the females curtsy and the males bow and give Her the Kiss of Fealty (right cheek). As they pass the High Priest, he hands each a white taper candle.

The High Priestess recites the Goddess Charge:

All ye assembled at mine shrine,
Mother Darksome and Divine.
Mine the Scourge and mine the Kiss,
Here I charge you in this sign.

(Assumes the Goddess position.)

All ye assembled in my sight,
Bow before my spirit bright.

(Coveners bow before High Priestess.)

Aphrodite, Arionhod,
Lover of the Horned God,
Mighty Queen of Witchery and night,
Morgan, Etoine, Nisene,
Diana, Bridgid, Melusine,
Am I named of old by men,
Artemis and Cerridwen,
Hell's dark mistress, Heaven's queen.
Ye who would ask of me a rune,
Or who would ask of me a boon,
Meet in in some secret glade,
Dance my round in greenwood shade,
By the light of the Full Moon.
In a place, wild and lone,
Dance about mine altar stone;
Work my holy mystery.
Ye who are feign to sorcery,
I bring ye secrets yet unknown.
No more shall ye know slavery,
Who give true worship unto me.
Ye who tread my round on Sabbat night,
Come ye naked to the rite,
In token that ye be really free.
I teach ye the mystery of rebirth,
Work ye my mysteries in mirth.
Heart joined to heart and lip to lip,
Five are the points of fellowship,
That bring ye ecstasy on earth,

For I am the circle of rebirth.
I ask no sacrifice, but do bow,
No other Law but love I know
By naught but love may I be known.
All things living are mine own,
From me they come, to me they go.

High Priest lights two altar candles and incense. Picks up altar candle and lights the Cauldron fire. High Priest assumes the God position. He recites the Invocation to the Horned God:

By the flame that burneth bright,
O Horned One!
We call Thy name into the night,
O Ancient One!
Thee we invoke, by the Moon-led sea,
By the standing stone and the twisted tree.
Thee we invoke, where gather Thine own,
By the nameless shore, forgotten and lone.
Come where the round of the dance is trod,
Horn and Hoof of the Goat Foot God!
By Moonlit meadow, on dusky hill,
When the haunted wood is hushed and still,
Come to the charm of the chanted prayer,
As the Moon bewitches the midnight air.
Evoke Thy powers that potent bide,
In shining stream and the secret tide.
In fiery flame by starlight pale
In shadowy host that rides the gale.
And by the ferndrakes, fairy haunted,

Of forests wild and woods enchanted,
Come? O Come!
To the heart-beat's drum!
Come to us who gather below,
When the broad white moon is climbing slow.
Through the stars to the heavens' height,
We hear Thy hoofs on the wind of night!
As black tree branches shake and sigh,
By joy and terror we know Thee nigh.
We speak the spell Thy power unlocks,
At Solstice, Sabbat, and Equinox!

The High Priest leads the coveners in a spiral dance that winds inward to the Cauldron, where each lights their taper at the Cauldron. Then the spiral unwinds. As the spiral dance is performed the High Priest and coveners chant:

EKO EKO AZARAK,
EKO EKO ZOMELEK,
EKO EKO ARIDA,
EKO EKO KERNUNNOS,
BEZABI, LACHA, BACHABABA.
LAMACH, CAHI, ACHABABA,
KARRELOS, CAHI, ACHABABA,
LAMACH LAMACH BACHAROUS,
CARBAHAJI, SABALYOS,
BARYLOS.
LAZOS, ATHAME, CALYOLAS,
SAMAHAC ET FAMYOLAS,
HARRAHYA!

High Priest leads the coveners in a dance around the High Priestess, Altar, Cauldron in a line just inside the Circle, chanting:

> *Darksome night and shining Moon,*
> *Hearken to the Witches' rune.*
> *East then South, West then North,*
> *Here! Come! I call Thee forth.*
> *By all the powers of land and sea,*
> *Be obedient unto me.*
> *Wand and Pentacle and sword,*
> *Hearken ye unto my word.*
> *Cords and Censer, Scourge and Knife,*
> *Waken all ye into life.*
> *Powers of the Witches' blade,*
> *Come ye as the charge is made.*
> *Queen of Heaven, Queen of Hell,*
> *Send your aid into the spell.*
> *Horned Hunter of the night,*
> *Work my will by magic rite.*
> *By all the powers of land and sea,*
> *As I do say, "So mote it be."*
> *By all the might of Moon and Sun,*
> *As I do will, it shall be done.*

End of chant and dance. High Priest and coveners salute, holding candles high. The High Priest says:

> *Behold the Great Mother*
> *Who hath brought forth*
> *The light of the world.*

EKO EKO ARIDA,
EKO EKO KERNUNNOS.

Kiss. The Coveners pass their tapers to the High Priest at the Altar, who returns them to the Altar, where they remain lighted.

High Priest returns candle to Altar and coveners file past the High Priestess and curtsy and males bow and give kiss. High Priestess blesses the cakes and wine and the Chalice is passed. The paten of cakes is passed and each partakes.

High Priest and High Priestess and coveners face North, East, South, and West and salute while the High Priest thanks the Ancient Ones and gives them license to depart the Circle.

This being a feast of the Waxing light of the Sun, the singing, games, dancing, and feasting after the rite is performed, last through the night and until the Sun's rays shine forth on the horizon. Then all witches go forth to welcome the Sun by standing in the morning Sunlight in a Greeting of Welcome. As the Sun's rays fall upon each covener, they bow and say:

EKO EKO ARIDA,
EKO EKO KERNUNNOS.

The Spring Sabbat
The Vernal Equinox
March 21

Green candles at four quarters. Silver candles on Altar
which is wreathed with spring flowers and a fire is prepared in the East within the Circle. High Priestess or
High Priest casts the Circle. High Priestess should read
The Charge with the coveners standing around the Circle alternately male-female.

> *All ye assembled at mine shrine,*
> *Mother Darksome and Divine.*
> *Mine the Scourge and mine the Kiss,*
> *Here I charge you in this sign.*

(Assumes God position.)

> *All ye assembled in my sight,*
> *Bow before my spirit bright.*

(Coveners bow before High Priestess.)

> *Aphrodite, Arionhod,*
> *Lover of the Horned God,*
> *Mighty Queen of Witchery and night,*
> *Morgan, Etoine, Nisene,*
> *Diana, Bridgid, Melusine,*
> *Am I named of old by men,*
> *Artemis and Cerridwen,*
> *Hell's dark mistress, Heaven's queen.*
> *Ye who would ask of me a rune,*
> *Or who would ask of me a boon,*
> *Meet me in some secret glade,*

Dance my round in greenwood shade,
By the light of the Full Moon.
In a place, wild and lone,
Dance about mine altar stone;
Work my holy mystery,
Ye who are feign to sorcery,
1 bring ye secrets yet unknown.
No more shall ye know slavery,
Who give true worship unto me.
Ye who tread my round on Sabbat night,
Come ye all naked to the rite,
In token that ye be really free.
I teach Ye the mystery of rebirth
Work ye my mysteries in mirth.
Heart joined to heart and lip to lip,
Five are the points of fellowship,
That bring ye ecstasy on earth,
For I am the circle of rebirth.
I ask no sacrifice, but do bow,
No other Law but love I know,
By naught but love may I be known,
All things living are mine own,
From me they come, to me they go.

High Priest stands in the East beside the unlit fire.
High Priestess stands facing High Priest holding Wand.

High Priestess:

We kindle this fire this day in the presence of
the Almighty Ones without malice, without
jealousy, without envy, without fear of ought

beneath the Sun but the High Gods. Thee we invoke, O Light of the Fire, O That which is Life. Be Thou as a bright flame before us, be Thou a smooth path between us, be Thou a guiding star above, kindle though within our hearts, a flame of love. For our neighbors, for our foes, to our neighbors, to our foes, to our friends, to our kindred all, to all men upon the broad earth. O Merciful Son of Cerridwen, from the lowliest thing that liveth, to the name that is Highest of all, Kernunnos.

The High Priestess then draws invoking Pentagram on the High Priest with her Wand then hands it to him with a kiss. High Priest lights fire. High Priestess and High Priest then lead the coveners around the Altar, leaping the flames as they reach them, until the fire begins to die down.

The coveners resume their places around the Altar. High Priest pours wine into the Quaich and High Priestess drinks. The High Priest drinks and passes Quaich around the coveners, each drinks, finishing with the High Priestess who drains it. This can be followed by dancing and games, cakes and wine if desired. Close Circle. Feast follows.

The Rudemas Sabbat

May Eve

April 30

Place green candles at the four cardinal points in the Circle. Place two white on the Altar. Decorate with spring flowers. High Priestess or High Priest casts the Magic Circle. All coveners are doubly purified. Dance around the Circle with Besoms chanting:

> *O do not tell the Priests of our Arts*
> *For they would call it sin;*
> *For we will be in the woods all night,*
> *A-conjuring Summer in.*
> *And bring you good news by word of mouth,*
> *For women, cattle and corn;*
> *For the Sun is a-coming up from the South*
> *With Oak and Ash and Thorn.*

Do the meeting dance, chanting:

> *EKO EKO AZARAK,*
> *EKO EKO ZOMELEK,*
> *EKO EKO ARIDA*
> *EKO EKO KERNUNNOS,*
> *BEZABI, LACHA, BACHABABA.*
> *LAMACH, CAHI, ACHABABA,*
> *KARRELOS, CAHI, ACHABABA,*
> *LAMACH LAMACH BACHAROUS,*
> *CARBAHAJI, SABALYOS,*
> *BARYLOS.*
> *LAZOS, ATHAME, CALYOLAS,*

SAMAHAC, ET FAMYOLAS,
HARRAHYA!

High Priestess assumes the God position. High Priest invokes and draws down the Moon. High Priest kneeling invokes:

> *I invoke Thee and call upon Thee, O Mighty*
> *Mother of us all, Bringer of all Fruitfulness,*
> *by seed and by root, by stem and by bud, by*
> *leaf and flower and fruit, by life and love, do*
> *I invoke Thee to descend upon the body of*
> *Thy Servant and High Priestess, (name)*
> *here.*

The sign of the 1, 2, 3 triangle is given to the High Priestess by all the men, all women bow. High Priest makes sign of the 1, 2, 3 triangle on High Priestess and concentrates his power upon her whilst kneeling at her feet and adoring.

All concentrate whilst High Priestess reads The Charge:

> *All ye assembled at mine shrine,*
> *Mother Darksome and Divine.*
> *Mine the Scourge and mine the Kiss,*
> *Here I charge you in this sign.*

(Assumes God position.)

> *All ye assembled in my sight,*
> *Bow before my spirit bright.*

(Coveners bow before High Priestess.)

Aphrodite, Arionhod,
Lover of the Horned God,
Mighty Queen of Witchery and night,
Morgan, Etoine, Nisene,
Diana, Bridgid, Melusine,
Am I named of old by men,
Artemis and Cerridwen,
Hell's dark mistress. Heaven's queen.
Ye who would ask of me a rune,
Or who would ask of me a boon,
Meet me in some secret glade,
Dance mv round in greenwood shade,
By the light of the Full Moon.
In a place, wild and lone,
Dance my round in greenwood shade,
By the light of the Full Moon.
In a place, wild and lone,
Dance about mine altar stone;
Work my holy mystery.
Ye who are feign to sorcery,
I bring ye secrets yet unknown.
No more shall ye know slavery,
Who give true worship unto me.
Ye who tread my round on Sabbat night,
Come ye all naked to the rite,
In token that ye be really free.
I teach ye the mystery of rebirth,
Work ye my mysteries in mirth.
Heart joined to heart and lip to lip,

Five are the points of fellowship,
That bring ye ecstasy on earth,
For I am the circle of rebirth.
I ask no sacrifice, but do bow,
No other Law but love I know,
By naught but love may I be known.
All things living are mine own,
From me they come, to me they go.

After effects of this ceremony are over, all should be purified in sacrifice before Her. She should then purify the High Priest and other men without partners with Her own hands. All partake of cakes and wine. Followed by feasting and singing, and dancing or fertility rites for good crops.

The Beltane Sabbat

The Summer Solstice

June 21

The Cauldron is wreathed with summer flowers and placed South of the Altar in the Magic Circle. A fire is built in it. The Magic Circle is cast and all are purified as usual.

The High Priestess assumes the God position while the High Priest, kneeling, invokes and draws down the Moon:

> *I invoke Thee and call upon Thee, O Mighty*
> *Mother of us all, Bringer of all Fruitfulness,*
> *by seed and by root, by stem and by bud, by*
> *leaf and flower and fruit, by life and by love*
> *do I invoke Thee to descend upon the body of*
> *Thy Servant and High Priestess, (name).*

All coveners concentrate while the High Priestess recites the Charge of the Goddess:

> *All ye assembled at mine shrine,*
> *Mother Darksome and Divine.*
> *Mine the Scourge and mine the Kiss,*
> *Here I charge you in this sign.*

(Assumes Goddess position.)

> *All ye assembled in my sight,*
> *Bow before my spirit bright.*

(Coveners bow before High Priestess.)

Aphrodite, Arionhod.
Lover of the Horned God,
Mighty Queen of Witchery and night,
Morgan, Etoine, Nisene,
Diana, Bridgid, Melusine,
Am I named of old by men,
Artemis and Cerridwen,
Hell's dark mistress, Heaven's queen.
Ye who would ask of me a rune,
Or who would ask of me a boon,
Meet in some secret glade,
Dance in my round in greenwood shade,
By the light of the Full Moon.
In a place, wild and lone
Dance about mine altar stone;
Work my holy mystery.
Ye who are feign to sorcery,
I bring ye secrets yet unknown.
No more shall ye know slavery,
Who give true worship unto me.
Ye who tread my round on Sabbat night,
Come ye all naked to the rite,
In token that ye be really free.
I teach ye the mystery of rebirth,
Work ye my mysteries in mirth.
Heart joined to heart and lip to lip,
Five are the points of fellowship,
That bring ye ecstasy on earth,
For I am the circle of rebirth.
I ask no sacrifice, but do bow,

No other Law but love I know,
By naught but love may I be known.
All things living are mine own,
From me they come, to me they go.

The High Priestess stands behind the Cauldron in the God position. The coveners file past, sunwise, alternately male-female. The men give her the sign of the 1, 2, 3 triangle and the Kiss of Fealty; the women bow to her. Then each takes a taper from the High Priest and lights it at the Cauldron. The High Priestess assumes the Goddess position, and the coveners walk slowly around the Magic Circle.

The High Priest recites:

Queen of the Moon,
Queen of the Stars,
Queen of the Horns,
Queen of the Fires,
Queen of the Earth,
Bring to us the Child of Promise!
For it is the Great Mother
Who gives birth to Him;
It is the Lord of Life
Who is born again.
Darkness and tears are set aside,
When the Sun comes up again.
Golden Sun of hill and mountain,
Illumine the world,
Illumine the Seas,
Illumine the rivers,

Illumine us all.
Grief be laid and joy be raised,
Blessed be the Great Mother!
Without beginning, without end,
Everlasting to Eternity.
Evoe! Io! Evoe! He!
Blessed Be! Blessed Be!

The High Priest then leads the dance around the High Priestess and the Altar to the Circle Chant. All chant:

EKO EKO AZARAK,
EKO EKO ZOMELEK,
EKO EKO ARIDA,
EKO EKO KERNUNNOS.
BEZABI, LACHA, BACHABABA.
LAMACH, CAHI, ACHABABA,
KARRELOS, CAHI, ACHABABA,
LAMACH LAMACH BACHAROUS,
CARBAHAJI, SABALYOS,
BARYLOS.
LAZOS, ATHAME, CALYOLAS,
SAMAHAC, ET FAMYOLAS,
HARRAHYA!

The High Priest gives the High Priestess the sign of the 1, 2, 3 triangle and the Kiss of Fealty. All men do likewise; the women bow.

After the ceremony there are cakes and wine, games and dancing.

The Lammas Sabbat
August 1

High Priestess or High Priest casts the Magic Circle. High Priestess at the Altar says:

> I (name) *High Priestess and Witch, do hereby invoke Thee O loving Arida, Mother of all things. As Thy Laws are, so shalt they be. Great is the Mother who has given us such tools as shall till the earth. Great is the Mother who has given us hands and a mouth for swallowing, who makest us grow without our knowledge and breathe whilst we are asleep.*

High Priestess salutes the four quarters. High Priestess says:

> *HEAR YE, O my people. The ploughland is heavy with the golden wheat of life, the cattle are bound, good substance fills the house, fair women are in their homes and with just laws good men rule in wealth and prosperity. The boys go gladly with the girls in flowing dances and gambol and frolic in the turf's sweet flowers.*

Coveners reply:

> *We hear thee, O Great Mother, and give thanks.*

High Priest salutes to the four quarters. High Priestess salutes to the four quarters and says:

> Hear ye, O my people, of the Power the Gods may give you. Remember this all those who have taken it upon themselves to have great powers, far greater than those of others, have incurred for a time hatred and unpopularity, but if one has to pursue a great aim this burden of envy must be accepted and it is wise to accept it. Hatred does not last forever, but the brilliance of the past is the glory of the future stored up in the memory of men. It is for you to safeguard against hatred and cherish that future glory and to do nothing now that is dishonorable. But first you must purify your mind and your body, saying to yourself, "Now it is my life I must shape as a carpenter shapes wood and the thing to be formed is a righteousness toward the Gods, as nothing is to me the body, and as nothing the parts thereof." Let death come when it will and I shall flee it not, for now they shall cast you out of the Universe. Wherever thou shall go there will be the Sun and the Moon and the Stars and Vision and Communion with the Gods.

Coveners reply:

> We hear ye, O Great Mother, and seek purity.

The Witches are then given a kiss, anointed and then scourged. The High Priestess is at the Altar chanting:

Mother of all things, come Thou beautiful
one, Only begotten Goddess of Light. Accept
these offerings we humbly give.

High Priest lights incense which Handmaiden hands to him. Fruits are presented and offered up. Wine is presented and offered up. Bread is presented and offered up.

High Priest says:

Hear, Blessed Goddess, we offer these fruits
of the Earth. Grant us in return abundant
health and prosperity and all the joys of life.
Ye, as Queen of all Delights, we ask.

High Priest and High Priestess lead dance around Altar with phallic riding poles or broomsticks, with Circle Chant:

EKO EKO AZARAK,
EKO EKO ZOMELEK,
EKO EKO ARIDA,
EKO EKO KERNUNNOS,
BEZABI, LACHA, BACHABABA.
LAMACH, CAHI, ACHABABA,
KARRELOS, CAHI, ACHABABA,
KARRELOS, CAHI, ACHABABA,
LAMACH LAMACH BACHAROUS,
CARBAHAJI, SABALYOS,
BARYLOS.

LAZOS, ATHAME, CALYOLAS,
SAMAHAC, ET FAMYOLAS,
HARRAHYA!

All coveners partake of cakes and wine and feast and dancing. Great Rite.

The Samhain Sabbat

The Autumnal Equinox

September 21

The Altar should be decorated with symbols of autumn: pine cones, oak sprigs, acorns, ripe ears of corn and dried leaves, autumn flowers, etc.

High Priest forms the Magic Circle. High Priest enters the Circle with the High Priestess. High Priestess purifies High Priest who returns scourging. Male coveners purify the female witches and they scourge the men in return. High Priest stands at the West side of the Altar in the God position.

High Priestess stands at the East side of the Altar facing the High Priest. High Priestess says:

> *Farewell O Sun, ever returning light,*
> *The Hidden God who ever yet remains,*
> *Who now departs to the Land of Youth.*
> *Through the Gates of Death,*
> *To dwell enthroned, the judge of Gods and men.*
> *Horned leader of the Hosts of Air,*
> *Yet ever as He stands unseen about the Circle,*
> *So dwelleth He within the Sacred Seed,*
> *The seed of newly ripened grain.*
> *Hidden in earth, the seed of the Stars,*
> *In Him is life and life is the Light of Man.*
> *That which was never born, can never die,*
> *So the Wicca weep not but rejoice.*

High Priestess draws near to High Priest and with a kiss gives him the phallic-tipped riding pole or broomstick. High Priest leads the dance with High Priestess who holds the sistrum, the witches following around the Altar chanting the Invocation to the Horned God.

By the flame that burneth bright,
O Horned One!
We call Thy name into the night,
O Ancient One!
Thee we invoke, by the Moon-led sea,
By the standing stone and the twisted tree.
Thee we invoke, where gather Thine own,
By the nameless shore, forgotten and lone.
Come where the round of the dance is trod,
Horn and Hoof of the Goat Foot God!
By moonlit meadow, on dusky hill,
When the haunted wood is hushed and still,
Come to the charm of the chanted prayer,
As the Moon bewitches the midnight air.
Evoke Thy powers that potent bide,
In shining stream and the secret tide.
In fiery flame by starlight pale,
In shadowy host that rides the gale.
And by the ferndrakes, fairy haunted,
Of forests wild and woods enchanted,
Come? O Come!
To the heart-beat's drum!
Come to us who gather below,
When the broad white Moon is climbing slow.

Through the stars to the heavens' height,
We hear Thy hoofs on the wind of night!
As black tree branches shake and sigh,
By joy and terror we know Thee nigh.
We speak the spell Thy power unlocks,
At Solstice, Sabbat, and Equinox!

High Priestess and High Priest and the Handmaiden perform the Blessing of the Cakes and Wine. The High Priestess dismisses the spirits of the Watchtowers and closes the Circle.

Dancing—any form that pleases the entire group. If hungry—eat.

The Hallowmas Sabbat

Halloween

October 31

All the coveners are properly prepared, naked and bound. All are purified by the Scourge. Prepare the place of worship. Place two black candles on the Altar. Place one red candle at the four corners (East, South, West, and North). A wreath of autumn flowers is on the Altar—the Crown of the Horned God is there also. The High Priest or the High Priestess forms the Magic Circle. Coveners enter the Circle. High Priest says:

> *O Gods, beloved of us all, Bless this our Sabbat that we, thy humble worshippers, may meet in love, joy, and bliss. Bless our rites this night with the presence of our departed kin.*

High Priest stands facing North with arms upraised and Sword held aloft. Coveners stand round him in semicircle holding hands. He then invokes the Horned God saying:

> *By the flame that burneth bright,*
> *O Horned One!*
> *We call Thy name into the night,*
> *O Ancient One!*
> *Thee we invoke, by the Moon-led sea,*
> *By the standing stone and the twisted tree.*
> *Thee we invoke, where gather Thine own,*
> *By the nameless shore, forgotten and lone.*

Come where the round of the dance is trod,
Horn and Hoof of the Goat Foot God!
By moonlit meadow, on dusky hill,
When the haunted wood is hushed and still,
Come to the charm of the chanted prayer,
As the Moon bewitches the midnight air.
Evoke Thy powers that potent bide,
In shining stream and the secret tide.
In fiery flame by starlight pale,
In shadowy host that rides the gale.
And by the ferndrakes, fairy haunted,
Of forests wild and woods enchanted,
Come? O Come!
To the heart-beat's drum!
Come to us who gather below,
When the broad White Moon is climbing slow.
Through the stars to the heavens' height,
We hear Thy hoofs on the wind of night!
As black tree branches shake and sigh,
By joy and terror we know Thee nigh.
We speak the spell Thy power unlocks,
At Solstice, Sabbat, and Equinox!

High Priest leads the High Priestess and coveners in the meeting dance. He with the riding pole held head upwards to represent the phallus. Slow dance to the Witches' Chant:

Darksome night and shining Moon,
Hearken to the Witches' rune.

East then South, West then North,
Here! Come! I call Thee forth.
By all the powers of land and sea,
Be obedient unto me.
Wand and Pentacle and Sword,
Hearken ye unto my word.
Cords and Censer. Scourge and Knife,
Waken all ye into life.
Powers of the Witches' Blade,
Come ye as the charge is made.
Queen of Heaven, Queen of Hell,
Send your aid unto the spell.
Horned Hunter of the night,
Work my will by magic rite.
By all the powers of land and sea,
As I do say, "So mote it be."
By all the might of Moon and Sun,
As I do will, it shall be done.

The High Priest and High Priestess invoke again.
High Priestess says:

Dread Lord of the Shadows, God of Life and
Bringer of Death. Yet as the knowledge of
Thee is Death, Open wide, I pray Thee, Thy
gates through all must pass. Let our dear
ones, who have gone before, return this night
to make merry with us. And when our time
comes, as it must, O Thou, the Comforter
and Consoler, The Giver of Peace and Rest,

we will enter Thy realm gladly and unafraid.
For we know that when rested and refreshed
among our dear ones, we will be reborn again
by Thy grace and that of the Lady Arida. Let
it be the same place and same time as our
dear ones, that we may love again. O Horned
One descend we pray on (name High Priest)
Thy High Priest and Witch.

High Priestess goes to High Priest and with pine-tipped Wand, draws an invoking Pentagram on his chest and on a wreath of autumn flowers on the Altar. High Priest kneels and High Priestess places ring (crown) of flowers on his head. Each witch is given a red taper lit from the candles on the Altar and large quantities of incense are scattered on the censer's burning ashes. High Priestess strikes the bell forty times with her Athame and says:

Hear Ye, my Witches,
Welcome to our Great Sabbat.
Welcome we the Spirits
Of our departed kin.

High Priestess strikes forty times on the bell again. Witches walk slowly around the Circle. High Priestess fills the Cup with wine and hands it to High Priest who drinks.

High Priest:

In humility, as the Horned One asks, I bid
my Witches drink.

High Priest takes the Cup to the first witch, giving it with the right hand whilst taking the taper with left and extinguishing. This is repeated with each witch.

High Priest says:

> *Listen, my Witches, to the words of the*
> *Horned One. Drink, dance and be merry in*
> *the presence of the Old Gods and the Spirits*
> *Of our departed kin.*

Coveners partake of the cakes and wine. Dances and games may be enjoyed by all. The Great Rite. Close the Circle. Merry Meet, Merry Part.